HEALING
RELATIONSHIPS
THROUGH FORGIVENESS

*REQUESTING GOD'S GRACE
FROM OTHERS*

A WORKBOOK COMPANION
FOR GROUP STUDY
PART 2

DONALD E. JONES, PHD

J & A BOOK PUBLISHERS
www.jabookpublishers.com

(C) 2016 Donald E. Jones, PhD

Printed in the United States of America

All rights reserved. No part of this book may be reproduced in any form without permission in writing from the author, except in the case of brief quotations embodied in critical articles or reviews.

All Scripture quotations are from the World English Bible. This version was selected because it is in the public domain and can be quoted without limit. A personal translation of a verse or passage will be designated with (DEJ).

ISBN-13: 978-0692741115
ISBN-10: 0692741119

DEDICATION

I dedicate this book to my Savior and Lord Jesus Christ. He has been with me every step of my journey upon the earth, and I so look forward to being in His presence forever and ever.

CONTENTS

Introduction	1
Chapter - 1. Ask Others Next	3
Chapter - 2. Humbly Make Restitution	9
Chapter - 3. Accept the Consequences	15
Chapter - 4. Gently Confront Sin	21
Conclusion	27

ACKNOWLEDGMENTS

I want to thank my wonderful and gracious wife Carol who has supported me in this ministry with sacrifice, enthusiasm, encouragement, and accountability. Most of all, she has been a constant blessing because of her willingness to listen. I was always sharing with her the truths God had been teaching me as I studied His word and wrote this book. It consumed many hours. Thank you, Carol, and I deeply love you.

I want to thank my son Gregory R. Jones for volunteering to be the primary editor of this important book. Without his time and effort in painstakingly and meticulously going over every word and every sentence checking and rechecking the sentence structure and grammar, I would not have been able to complete it. Thank you for your ministry to me. I love you my son.

I want to thank my other children, Krista, Matt, and Kara for their love for Christ and His Word and their willingness to live for Him. I love you all.

A WORKBOOK COMPANION FOR GROUP STUDY PART 2

Introduction

This workbook is designed to aid in the comprehension and application of the truths from the Scriptures which are found in the book of the same name. It has a question and answer format because asking questions was a powerful teaching method that the Lord used to reveal God's divine truth. Jesus asked over one hundred and thirty questions as He instructed the people of God and others. These are only the recorded ones. We can only speculate as to how many questions He might have actually asked. The Lord used His questioning techniques to prompt His listeners to focus, understand, analyze, evaluate, and apply the principles He was proclaiming to them. The same has been done in this workbook.

In Matthew 17, Jesus enters the town of Capernaum after a long absence. This was a perfect opportunity for the tax-collectors to make some money and see if Jesus was paying his share of the taxes. These were Jewish tax collectors who obtained money for the support of the temple. The people of the town would have known Jesus and His disciples well since Peter's home and the town functioned as their base of operations. When they saw Peter, they approached him and asked if Jesus had paid the temple taxes. It was the drachma which was two days wages. Peter responded with a "yes." Then, Peter went into the house to ask the Lord if they actually had paid them. He was perplexed. He may have been thinking, "Do we pay taxes or not?" Or, he may have thought "Why do we have to pay taxes when we are citizens of heaven?"

Matthew states that Jesus knew exactly what was on his mind. As a result, Jesus asked one of His defining questions to direct Peter to the correct answer. At the end of verse 25,

REQUESTING GOD'S GRACE FROM OTHERS

Matthew records this, "When he came into the house, Jesus anticipated him, saying, "What do you think, Simon? From whom do the kings of the earth receive toll or tribute? From their children or from strangers?" To assist Peter, Jesus asks Peter if a king has his own sons (family members) pay taxes or does he have strangers do it. The answer is obvious the king receives taxes from strangers for his sons. So Peter responds, "Strangers." Then, at the end of verse 26, Jesus explains, "Therefore the children are exempt."

Here Jesus is referring to God the Father as the king of the temple and He as His Son. Therefore as His Son, He does not have to pay taxes because the King (God) collects taxes for His Son (Jesus). Jesus is exempt. Yet, the Lord will pay it anyway. Why? He doesn't want to offend them. He doesn't want the gospel hindered in the eyes of the tax-collectors and the people. At the beginning of verse 27, the Lord says, "But, lest we cause them to stumble."

Here is a perfect opportunity to teach a truth and perform a miracle. At the end of the verse 27, Jesus commands Peter, "Go to the sea, cast a hook, and take up the first fish that comes up. When you have opened its mouth, you will find a stater [different coin, same amount] coin. Take that, and give it to them for me and you." This is exactly what happened. The taxes were miraculously paid. Jesus used a question to aid Peter in his thinking process concerning the tax. As Jesus used questions, so shall we. May the questions in this book help you focus, understand, analyze, evaluate, and apply these biblical principles.

Chapter 1

Ask Others Next

We constantly ask God for forgiveness and are forgiven by Him and He desires that we do the same toward others. This pattern of confessing and forgiving is His blueprint.

In the section, "A Typical Scenario," the author describes an encounter with a father who has wrongfully accused his own daughter of denting the car and will not ask her for forgiveness.

What is the scenario about?

What did the conflict concern?

What was the relationship between the parties?

Have you had a similar experience?

REQUESTING GOD'S GRACE FROM OTHERS

In the section, "A Scriptural Principle" the author presents an important biblical principle in the forgiveness process which concerns asking others for forgiveness.

How would you express this principle in your own words?

How would you rewrite this principle to make it even more personal to your life (using your name and situation)?

Why do you think this principle might be important in your life right now?

How would you rate yourself on the percentage of times you followed this principle in the past when you did something wrong in a relationship?

Directions: Put a horizontal mark and your name where you see yourself on the percentage line.

| 0%   25%   50%   75%   100% |

A WORKBOOK COMPANION FOR GROUP STUDY PART 2

In the section, "A Biblical Explanation," the author explains the reasons why we are to ask for forgiveness when we sin against others in a relationship and how to do it.

What is the Lord God's usual pattern of dealing with sin in our relationship with Him?

According to Romans 2:15, what is inside all people which instinctively prompts them to ask others for forgiveness?

In the incident between Abimelech and Abraham, who was the one who asked for forgiveness and why?

In incident between Pharaoh and Moses, who was the one who asked for forgiveness and why?

In the incident between Nabal and David, who was the one who asked for forgiveness and why?

In what ways might these truths impact your relationships?

REQUESTING GOD'S GRACE FROM OTHERS

In the section, "An Ancient Portrait," the author describes the sin of Joseph's brothers against him and the circumstances that led them to ask him for forgiveness.

What was the brothers' sin against Joseph and why did they do it?

When Joseph met his brothers many years later, how did he demonstrate that he had already forgiven them?

What happened to make his brothers fearful that Joseph may have not forgiven them and would retaliate?

Since the brothers were fearful of facing Joseph directly, how did they ask him for forgiveness?

What was Joseph's response to their gesture?

Have you ever been in a situation that was comparable to either Joseph having to forgive a harsh sin or his brothers who needed to ask for forgiveness? How was it different and how was it the same?

A WORKBOOK COMPANION FOR GROUP STUDY PART 2

In the section, "A Modern Anecdote," the author explains how two parents impulsively divorced and discovered that they had to ask for forgiveness from their children.

According to Proverbs, what was the initial step the parents had to take to resolve their divorce issues?

Why was it so important for each spouse to ask the other for forgiveness?

Why was it important for the parents ask their children for forgiveness?

How would the asking of forgiveness by the parents affect their children's future?

After the parents asked the children for forgiveness what did the children have to do and why?

Based on the truths learned in this chapter, what would you have done differently if you were one of the parents or one of the children?

REQUESTING GOD'S GRACE FROM OTHERS

In the section, "A Personal Response," the author provides a model you may use for prayer if you find it necessary after discovering the truths in this chapter.

Are you presently in a relationship where you have sinned against another and have not asked God for forgiveness? If not, is there one from the past that still needs this prayer to be prayed?

Based on the truths you have just learned, what will you continue doing in your current relationships and what will you do differently?

What additional thoughts would you like to share with the others?

Chapter 2

Humbly Make Restitution

There may be times when we should make restitution to those we have wronged. This is not a part of forgiveness on their part but a part of repentance on ours.

In the section, "A Typical Scenario," the author describes an incident where a husband and wife disagree and may need to reconcile.

What is the scenario about?

What did the conflict concern?

What was the relationship between the parties?

Have you had a similar experience?

REQUESTING GOD'S GRACE FROM OTHERS

In the section, "A Scriptural Principle" the author presents an important biblical principle in the forgiveness process which concerns making restitution toward those we have wronged.

How would you express this principle in your own words?

How would you rewrite this principle to make it even more personal to your life (using your name and situation)?

Why do you think this principle might be important in your life right now?

How would you rate yourself on the percentage of times you followed this principle in the past when you did something wrong in a relationship?

Directions: Put a horizontal mark and your name where you are on the pecentage line.

| 0% | 25% | 50% | 75% | 100% |

A WORKBOOK COMPANION FOR GROUP STUDY PART 2

In the section, "A Biblical Explanation," the author explains the reasons why we should demonstrate repentance through restitution when we sin against others and how to do it.

What is the relationship of restitution to our repentance and forgiveness?

According to Leviticus 6:5, how much restitution should be made and when?

According to 1 Samuel 25, how did Abigail make restitution to David for the foolishness of her husband Nabal?

What was David's response to her actions?

In what two parables is restitution presented by Jesus?

In what ways might these truths impact your relationships?

REQUESTING GOD'S GRACE FROM OTHERS

In the section, "An Ancient Portrait," the author shares the story of the salvation of Zacchaeus and his great desire to make restitution to those he had cheated.

How did tax-collectors get paid?

How did tax-collectors usually mistreat people?

What were the reactions of the people who were cheated?

When Zacchaeus believed in the Lord Jesus, what restitution did he desire to make?

How might restitution affect our relationship with those we have wronged?

Have you ever been in a situation comparable to Zacchaeus or those he wronged? How was it different and how was it the same?

A WORKBOOK COMPANION FOR GROUP STUDY PART 2

In the section, "A Modern Anecdote," the author describes how a mother wronged her daughter and wanted to make restitution.

What was the mother's problem and how did she get herself into it?

What were the consequences of the mother's wrongdoing?

After her repentance, how did the mother want to make the necessary restitution?

Why did the husband want to make restitution to his wife and how was he going to do it?

Why did the daughter want to make restitution to her mom and how was she going to do it?

Based on the truths learned in this chapter, what would you have done differently if you were the husband, mother, or daughter?

REQUESTING GOD'S GRACE FROM OTHERS

In the section, "A Personal Response," the author provides a model you may use for prayer if you find it necessary after discovering the truths in this chapter.

Are you presently in a relationship where you have sinned against another and have not asked God for forgiveness? If not, is there one from the past that still needs this prayer to be prayed?

Based on the truths you have just learned, what will you continue doing in your current relationships and what will you do differently?

What additional thoughts would you like to share with the others?

Chapter 3

Accept the Consequences

When we sin in relationships, we accept the consequences as God trains us to be more like Him. These may come from God, parents, spouses, friends, bosses, churches, or the law.

In the section, "A Typical Scenario," the author describes an incident where someone forgot a task and refused to accept the consequences.

What is the scenario about?

What did the conflict concern?

What was the relationship between the parties?

Have you had a similar experience?

REQUESTING GOD'S GRACE FROM OTHERS

In the section, "A Scriptural Principle" the author presents an important biblical principle in the forgiveness process which concerns our acceptance of the consequences for our sin.

How would you express this principle in your own words?

How would you rewrite this principle to make it even more personal to your life (using your name and situation)?

Why do you think this principle might be important in your life right now?

How would you rate yourself on the percentage of times you followed this principle in the past when you did something wrong in a relationship?

Directions: Put a horizontal mark and your name where you are on the pecentage line.

| 0%   25%   50%   75%   100%

A WORKBOOK COMPANION FOR GROUP STUDY PART 2

In the section, "A Biblical Explanation," the author explains the reasons why we should demonstrate repentance through accepting the consequences when we sin against others.

How is restitution related to accepting the consequences for our actions?

If someone has difficulty forgiving us, could this problem be a consequence for our wrongdoing in the relationship and why?

How does God use consequences to train us to have stronger relationships?

How would the government become involved in providing consequences for actions in a relationship?

What are two Biblical examples of God directly providing the consequences for sin?

In what ways might these truths impact your relationships?

REQUESTING GOD'S GRACE FROM OTHERS

In the section, "An Ancient Portrait," the author describes the prodigal son's desire to accept the consequences for his sin.

In what way did the younger son transgress his father and then his older brother?

How did the father respond in love?

What critical event drove the prodigal son to finally repent?

What action did the prodigal son want to take in order to accept the consequences for his sin?

Do you think the prodigal son received back all the money he had spent and why?

Have you ever been in a situation comparable to the son's desire to accept the consequences or the father's willingness to forgive?

A WORKBOOK COMPANION FOR GROUP STUDY PART 2

In the section, "A Modern Anecdote," the author discusses a situation where one roommate needed to set consequences for another who was being irresponsible.

What two words might characterize the kind of relationship John and Steve had?

What did Steve do to break his relationship with John?

How did Steve display over and over his irresponsibility to John when they were growing up?

What plan did John put into place for Steve to become more responsible for his actions?

Once John had initiated the plan, what was he now free to do?

Based on the truths learned in this chapter, what would you have done differently if you were John or Steve?

REQUESTING GOD'S GRACE FROM OTHERS

In the section, "A Personal Response," the author provides a model you may use for prayer if you find it necessary after discovering the truths in this chapter.

Are you presently in a relationship where you have sinned against another and have not asked God for forgiveness? If not, is there one from the past that still needs this prayer to be prayed?

Based on the truths you have just learned, what will you continue doing in your current relationships and what will you do differently?

What additional thoughts would you like to share with the others?

Chapter 4

Gently Confront Sin

If others sin against us or we sin against them, we are to take our responsibility first for what we have done and then gently confront them.

In the section, "A Typical Scenario," the author describes an encounter between neighbors that resulted in a torn dress shirt and would require a reconciliation.

What is the scenario about?

What did the conflict concern?

What was the relationship between the parties?

Have you had a similar experience?

REQUESTING GOD'S GRACE FROM OTHERS

In the section, "A Scriptural Principle" the author presents an important biblical principle in the forgiveness process which concerns gently confronting others for their sin.

How would you express this principle in your own words?

How would you rewrite this principle to make it even more personal to your life (using your name and situation)?

Why do you think this principle might be important in your life right now?

How would you rate yourself on the percentage of times you followed this principle in the past when you did something wrong in a relationship?

Directions: Put a horizontal mark and your name where you are on the percentage line.

0%   25%   50%   75%   100%

A WORKBOOK COMPANION FOR GROUP STUDY PART 2

In the section, "A Biblical Explanation," the author explains the reasons why we are to gently confront those who have sinned against us in a relationship and how to do it.

What is the primary and most important purpose of gently confronting others?

In the discussion of the second and third purposes, once we know the facts, what does each party do?

The fourth purpose is to gain back your brother. What does this mean?

According to the fifth purpose, what positive result could arise from the gentle confrontation of an unbeliever?

According to the sixth purpose, what is the Devil's snare of an unbeliever that gentle confrontation can eliminate?

In what ways might these truths impact your relationships?

REQUESTING GOD'S GRACE FROM OTHERS

In the section, "An Ancient Portrait," the author describes the confrontation of the Lord Jesus by Martha concerning Mary and His response.

What was the conflict between Mary and Martha?

In what three ways did Martha improperly confront Mary?

Why had Martha become so upset about the tasks that she had taken on?

How did the Lord Jesus properly confront Martha after she had improperly confronted Him?

Why did the Lord Jesus take a stand against Martha rather than simply surrender to her demands?

Have you ever been in a situation comparable to Martha's demands, Mary's choice, or Jesus' stand and how was it the same and how was it different?

A WORKBOOK COMPANION FOR GROUP STUDY PART 2

In the section, "A Modern Anecdote," the author discusses a situation in which a young woman developed unhealthy eating habits in response to her sister's criticism.

How did the young lady's eating problems begin?

How did the author immediately deal with her self-esteem problem?

Why did her older sister have to be gently confronted and what was the result?

Why did her parents have to be gently confronted and what was the result?

Why did the young lady have to be gently confronted by her parents and what was the result?

Based on the truths learned in this chapter, what would you have done differently if you were young lady who was being criticized, the older sister with all the responsibility, or the parents who were so concerned?

REQUESTING GOD'S GRACE FROM OTHERS

In the section, "A Personal Response," the author provides a model you may use for prayer if you find it necessary after discovering the truths in this chapter.

Are you presently in a relationship where you have sinned against another and have not asked God for forgiveness? If not, is there one from the past that still needs this prayer to be prayed?

Based on the truths you have just learned, what will you continue doing in your current relationships and what will you do differently?

What additional thoughts would you like to share with the others?

Conclusion

As we conclude this book, I would like to leave us with some final thoughts about our God of forgiveness and what His Son did on the cross for us. First, if we understand the full extent of what was wrought for us on that cursed tree in order to forgive us, it will become so much easier to do the same thing for others. Second, if you read this entire book and realized that you do not understand salvation or have never received Christ as Lord and Savior, then I would like to provide that opportunity. Please do not skip this section; it may be the most important in your life.

From all outward appearances, humans seem "good" and attempt to live decent lives. This is man's concept of himself. This is not God's concept. The Almighty's view is that people all over the world and throughout the ages sin, sin, and sin again (Romans 3:23). This is a terrible and utterly destructive condition. Yet, they have ramifications that are far worse. These sins condemn us to everlasting divine retribution.

Though described briefly in the Old Testament, the Lord Jesus Christ clearly announced and proclaimed the future punishment to come. Contrary to popular belief, Jesus did not only speak of love, grace, and mercy, He also spoke of the coming judgment for sin. He declared that the judgment of sin would be everlasting punishment in a place He called "Hell." The Lord portrayed this place as an eternal inferno (Matthew 18:8) where there would be the weeping (from the sorrow) and gnashing of teeth (from the agony and anguish of suffering) continually into eternity (Matthew 8:12; 13:42, 50; 22:13; 24:51; 25:30; Luke 13:28).

Why must people face this horrific punishment? Though God is a God of love, grace, and mercy, He is also a God of great holiness, righteousness, and justice (Psalm 89:14,18). These attributes are just as much a part of His divine nature as His love, grace, and mercy. You have broken God's law as we all have and the penalty must be paid. This began with the first man Adam (Genesis 3:1-7). When this occurred, His love, grace, and mercy surfaced and a provision was made. Someone else would have to take man's place and pay the penalty. Someone who had never transgressed Him, who would never deserve punishment, and would fulfill all of God's Laws, would be substituted in man's place. This was the Son of God, Jesus Christ.

As the God-Man, He would pay the penalty for our sins in His death on the cross. Once done, the Lord God made only one provision for people to appropriate what His Son had done on the cross for them. This provision is receiving Jesus Christ as Savior and Lord. Though I cannot possibly share with you this good news in the confines of this book, I would love for you to consider purchasing my book entitled, *Finding The Light: The Kingdom of Heaven and How To Enter It*. It can be found for sale on Amazon.com. It is inexpensive and contains the full gospel message for your consideration. This message is so important and extensive that it cannot adequately be contained in a few pages at the end of a book.

If you are a believer, you must go out into the world and forgive as you are forgiven. These principles are to be lived and shared with others. You now have the tools to make your relationships last a lifetime. Go live them out and share them with others!

ABOUT THE AUTHOR

Dr. Donald Jones is currently a Christian Pastoral Counselor with thirty-eight years of experience in the fields of pastoral ministry, public education, and Christian counseling. He carries degrees and certificates from four major universities and from a variety of educational institutions. He has been a professor of Languages and Bible, a television commentator, and a featured speaker at a variety of events and seminars at churches, schools, and other organizations across the United States. He is a member in good standing of several secular and Christian professional organizations. Dr. Jones has been a published author since 1976. For further information view his website at www.donjonesphd.com.

www.ingramcontent.com/pod-product-compliance
Lightning Source LLC
Chambersburg PA
CBHW030313030426
42337CB00012B/697